THE BECKET LEAVES

Janet Backhouse
and
Christopher de Hamel

THE BRITISH LIBRARY

© 1988 The British Library Board

First published 1988 by
The British Library, Great Russell Street
London WC1B 3DG

British Library Cataloguing in Publication Data

Backhouse, Janet
    The Becket leaves.
    1. England. Becket, Thomas, Saint –
    Biographies
    I. Title   II. de Hamel, Christopher
    942.03′1′0924

ISBN 0 7123 0141 0

The British Library is grateful to the following for
permission to reproduce certain items: the Masters
and Fellows of Trinity College Cambridge (fig.1);
Sotheby's (fig.2); the Syndics of Cambridge
University Library (fig.10).

Designed by James Shurmer

Typeset in 10½/15 pt Linotron 202 Bembo
by Bexhill Phototypesetters, Bexhill-on-Sea

Colour origination by York House Graphics, Hanwell
Printed in England on Skyesilk 135 gm^2 toned matt art
by The Roundwood Press, Warwick

PREFACE

by Lord Quinton, Chairman, the British Library Board

In June 1986 a four-leaf fragment from a 13th-century verse Life of St Thomas Becket, illustrated with coloured drawings, was offered for sale at Sotheby's in London. The leaves, which had been in a private collection in Belgium for at least 150 years, were already known to scholars from a set of black and white reproductions published in 1885 and they had always been recognised as English work. However, no-one had had an opportunity to study the originals in detail in more recent times, and the quality and freshness of the drawings far exceeded expectations based on old photographs. After an exciting struggle in the saleroom, where bidding rose to almost £1.4 million (the highest price ever paid for any English book), the fragment was bought on behalf of J. Paul Getty, KBE who, anxious that this unfamiliar treasure should become as widely known as possible in its country of origin, placed it on indefinite loan in the British Library and has encouraged exhibition and publication.

A worrying aspect of the excitement created by the sale of the Becket Leaves was the fact that, since they were held outside the country, there was no way in which the danger of their being bought by an overseas buyer and so irrecoverably lost to Britain could be circumvented. The level of the price they reached put them beyond the resources of the British Library. We are extremely grateful for the generosity of Mr Getty in letting us house and exhibit the treasure he has acquired in the country from which it came and to whose history it refers.

The story of Becket and his former friend Henry II is a crucial ingredient in our national myth, kept alive for many by T. S. Eliot's *Murder In The Cathedral* and for even more, no doubt, by the film made from Jean Anouilh's play. The leaves stand to the killing of Becket in the relation of the Bayeux Tapestry to the Norman Conquest, clothing an event of great national significance in authoritative imagery. This volume will serve to put the leaves in an intelligible setting in an expert way and will also be an inducement to come and see the original work itself.

1 An illuminated Gospels from Becket's own library, which he commissioned in France and brought back with him in 1170. The archbishop depicted in the roundel below the figure of Christ is probably intended to represent Becket himself. Cambridge, Trinity College, MS. B. 5. 5, f.130v.

ST THOMAS BECKET

The conflict between Henry II and Thomas Becket is one of the greatest stories in history. The assassination of Thomas Becket in Canterbury Cathedral on 29 December 1170 was probably the first event in English history to have an immediate and still relevant influence on European affairs.

The four Becket Leaves were once part of a popularised version of the life of England's most famous saint, designed for private enjoyment rather than for formal use. The text is in French, the fashionable language of polite society in medieval England, and the lively illustrations, full of fascinating contemporary detail, transform episodes from the story into something approaching a modern strip cartoon. There is one of the earliest pictures of an English coronation, and an important scene of a royal feast complete with early gothic metalwork and with a minstrel playing a harp. There are detailed pictures of three ships with features of their construction clearly delineated. There are drawings of soldiers, armour, swords, lances, seven horses, chairs, a bed, and costumes of all classes from king and pope to peasant. Unfortunately the bulk of the book has been lost and the surviving pages cover only a part of the period which Becket spent in exile in France towards the end of his career.

The French poem is based on the formal Latin Lives of Becket which were written soon after his martyrdom in 1170. The facts of his life and death are better recorded than those of any other medieval Englishman. The authors of the earliest accounts were his personal friends and colleagues or were closely associated with members of his immediate entourage. Among them were John of Salisbury, a life-long friend and the leading English man of letters of the day, and Herbert of Bosham, the principal scholar in Becket's own household. Extracts from their accounts, and from those of William of Canterbury and Alan of Tewkesbury, were brought together to form the *Quadrilogus,* an 'official' Latin biography of the saint, the first version of which was available as early as 1199. John of Salisbury and William of Canterbury were both in Canterbury Cathedral when Becket was assassinated. So too were William Fitzstephen and Edward Grim, who contributed their own descriptions of events and who also commanded a wide readership.

The historical figure who emerges from all these accounts was a lively and forceful personality, fond of sports and a connoisseur of horses, who enjoyed the privileges and ceremonies that accompanied the high offices he held. Among the tangible relics that have come down to us are a number of the beautifully illuminated books which were collected for his private library and one of these includes a tiny image of a figure in archiepiscopal dress that must surely be intended to represent Becket himself (fig. 1). He owed his sainthood not to any particular holiness of life, though during his years as Archbishop he is said to have practised some personal austerities, but entirely to the fact that he died violently in the cause of his church, upholding its rights in the face of encroachment by the secular power of an individual state.

The struggle between the absolute monarchy of Henry and the immovable religious principle of St Thomas brought two quite exceptional men into headlong confrontation. It is interpreted here as the great medieval crisis in the ageless debate between liberty and despotism. Thomas Becket is seen as the champion of freedom: he is shown here as the supporter of the *vulgus* (f.2v), the common people, against autocracy – a theme which in England culminated first in Magna Carta in 1215, drafted by Becket's successor Stephen Langton and sealed by Henry's son, King John, and this theme is chillingly relevant in parts of the modern world.

Becket was appointed Archbishop of Canterbury in 1162 at the insistence of King Henry II, in spite of his own strongly expressed reservations. Although at the time he had yet to be ordained priest, he had enjoyed years of experience in church affairs as a member of the household of his predecessor, Archbishop Theobald. He had also served and supported the king for seven years as Chancellor, combining his political role with that of close personal friend and adviser. Each successive Archbishop of Canterbury had an important statesman's role to play within the kingdom, especially during the king's frequent and often protracted absences in his continental lands. Becket seemed a perfect choice for the primacy of England and Henry II anticipated that the appointment would ensure the co-operation of the church in his personal scheme for law and government. But he had failed to recognise his friend's exceptional capacity for identification with the interests of whatever position he might be called upon to fill, regardless of earlier loyalties. When Becket the Archbishop saw a conflict between the interests of the church he now represented and the state which his king confidently expected him to serve, Henry found himself implacably opposed by the very man who, as Becket the Chancellor, would have given him unqualified support. Although Becket was forced into exile in 1164 and returned to England six years later apparently reconciled with Henry but in fact only to face death, the king was eventually obliged, as part of his expiation of the murder of the Archbishop, to give way on those matters over which Becket had opposed him.

Thomas Becket died on 29 December 1170, cut down within the walls of his own cathedral by four knights whose action was directly inspired by the words and deeds of the king. Within weeks of the event visions and miracles were reported from the simple tomb in the desecrated cathedral where his mutilated corpse had hurriedly been laid. Within months the first accounts of the life of the new martyr were in circulation. News of his dramatic and violent end spread rapidly throughout Christendom, following trade routes, pilgrim roads and the march of the Crusaders to the Holy Land. An international enthusiasm for his cult was facilitated by England's wide connections with the rest of Europe, particularly in western France, where Henry II's lands extended from the Channel to the Pyrenees, and in Saxony, northern Spain and Sicily, where his three daughters had contracted political marriages. The English also played a prominent role in the Crusader campaigns, especially during the reign of Henry's immediate successor, Richard the Lionheart. A military order, the Knights of St Thomas of Acre, was founded

2 Henry II's daughter Matilda and her husband Henry, Duke of Saxony crowned by God. Henry II and his mother, the Empress Matilda, stand behind the Duchess and Becket, holding a martyr's palm, is included immediately above them. This miniature was painted within two decades of Becket's death. The Gospels of Henry the Lion, f.171v.

in Becket's honour as early as 1190 and had its English headquarters in London on the site of the saint's family home in Cheapside, now occupied since the Reformation by the hall of the Mercers' Company. The four knights responsible for Becket's death, Hugh de Morville, William de Tracy, Reginald Fitzurse and Richard le Breton, were sentenced by the Pope to spend fourteen years fighting in the Holy Land as part of their personal penance for the murder.

Popular acclaim was quickly followed by official recognition. On 21 February 1173 the Pope pronounced Becket's canonisation. In July of the following year Henry II himself came humbly to Canterbury to enact a scene of public penance at the shrine. A major rebuilding programme following a disastrous fire in the east end of the cathedral in 1174 was utilised to provide a superb setting for Becket's relics, which were translated into their new resting place amid ceremonies of the utmost splendour on 7 July 1220. For

3 The martyrdom of Becket. A miniature from the Hastings Hours, written and illuminated in Flanders about 1480. Additional MS 54782, f.55v.

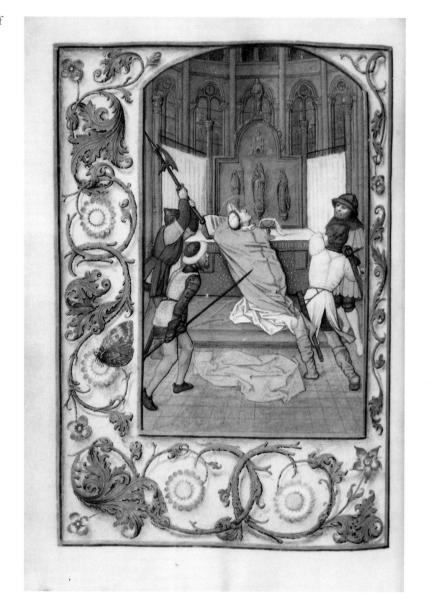

4 A group of pilgrims on the road. An early 16th-century miniature introducing Lydgate's 'Story of Thebes', which was written as an addition to *The Canterbury Tales*. Royal MS 18 D. ii, f.148.

5 The martyrdom of Becket. A marginal illustration from the Luttrell Psalter, painted about 1325–35. It has been defaced by lines scored through the figure of the Archbishop, probably at the time of the Reformation. Additional MS 42130, f.51.

three-and-a-half centuries the pilgrimage to Canterbury was among the most popular in Europe and an unending succession of miracles was attributed to Becket's intercession.

Chaucer's *Canterbury Tales,* written in the late 1380s, preserves for us something of the flavour of this popular medieval excursion. Adopting the fashionable device of linking an anthology of stories by assigning them to members of a group of people with a common interest – a device used also by Boccaccio in his *Decameron* – Chaucer describes a variety of personalities, attitudes and aspirations that could plausibly be found among an organised group of English pilgrims comfortably taking the road to Becket's shrine (fig. 4). A customary of the shrine, drawn up in 1428 by its two custodians, records the practical observances which these pilgrims would have experienced at the end of their journey, giving an overall picture of a meticulously organised religious and tourist institution and industry. Detailed instructions for solemn services and less formal devotions due to St Thomas are coupled with precise directions for the opening hours of the precincts of the shrine and for the expenditure of some of the very considerable revenues derived from it. The survival in large numbers of souvenir lead badges portraying Becket, Canterbury bells for horse bridles, and miniature ampullae designed to contain holy water sanctified by contact with the saint's blood reflect the humbler commercial aspects of the operation.

In the early years of the 16th century Henry VIII was not slow to realise that Becket's example could become a rallying point for opposition to his own assertions of supremacy over the church. He was not alone in seeing possible parallels between events in his own reign and the events which culminated in Becket's death in 1170. In 1530 his own Archbishop of Canterbury, William Warham, drafted a speech for the House of Lords in which he declared himself to stand for the principles for which his sainted predecessor had died. It is not therefore surprising that Henry should have addressed himself particularly to the extermination of the shrine and cult of Becket, proclaiming on 16 November 1538 that '. . . from henceforth the said Thomas Becket shall not be esteemed, named, reputed nor called a Saint, but Bishop Becket, and that his images and pictures through the whole realm shall be put down and avoided out of all churches, chapels and all other places: and

Pilgrim badges: (left) Head of St Thomas Becket. Lead. 14th century. British Museum. *(centre)* Becket on horseback. Lead. 14th century. British Museum. *(right)* Becket flanked by two of his assassins. An ampulla for holy water. Lead. 13th century. British Museum.

that henceforth the days used to be a festival in his name shall not be observed, nor the service, office, antiphons, collects and prayers in his name read, but erased and put out of all the books'. The erasures and mutilations enjoined by this proclamation are commonly to be seen in surviving medieval service books and provide a clear indication of each such book's presence in England at the time of the Reformation (fig. 5).

Although the Becket Leaves represent a unique survival of a cycle of illustrations attached to a written Life of Becket, individual pictures of him and of incidents relating to his life and death proliferated between the late 12th century and the Reformation. Among the earliest large scale examples are a mosaic figure in the cathedral of Monreale in Sicily and a sequence of wall paintings dating from about 1226 in Brunswick cathedral in Lower Saxony. The first known English miniature of the martyrdom, with related scenes, was probably painted about 1180 and appears in an early copy of John of Salisbury's Life of Becket which was made at the Augustinian abbey of Cirencester (PLATE 1). Two very fine late 12th-century miniatures of the saint's death and burial, inserted in a slightly later

6 King Ecgfrith exhorting St Cuthbert to leave his hermitage and accept a bishopric. A miniature from Bede's Life of St Cuthbert, written and illuminated for Durham cathedral priory about 1200. Yates Thompson MS 26, f.51.

7 (*left*) St Guthlac taking leave of his fellow warriors. A tinted drawing from the Guthlac Roll, made early in the 13th century. Harley Roll Y.6.

7 (*right*) St Guthlac ferried by fishing boat to the Lincolnshire island of Crowland, where he lived as a hermit in the late 7th century. A tinted drawing from the Guthlac Roll, made early in the 13th century. Harley Roll Y.6.

psalter of English workmanship, must also have been painted within about a quarter of a century of the martyrdom (PLATES II and III). Thereafter miniatures depicting Becket's death are increasingly common in devotional books designed for the English market, though other scenes are rare. The longest surviving manuscript cycle is a series of 22 delicately tinted marginal drawings in Queen Mary's Psalter, written and illuminated possibly in London at the beginning of the 14th century (PLATES IV and V). This sequence includes the romantic legend of Becket's parentage. His mother was popularly reputed to have been the daughter of a Saracen emir who, meeting the Crusader knight Gilbert Becket while he was held captive by her father, fell passionately in love with him and followed him to England where she was baptised a Christian and duly became his wife.

Illustrated lives of individual saints survive in considerable numbers from medieval England. A beautifully illuminated copy of Bede's Life of St Cuthbert was made for Durham cathedral priory at the end of the 12th century (fig. 6). Episodes from the story of St Guthlac of Croyland were set out in roundels in the unusual form of a pictorial roll early in the 13th century (fig. 7). By the second quarter of the 13th century a much increased demand for books for individual use encouraged the production of increasing numbers of picture books. Accounts of the lives of popular saints and other historical characters provided material suitable for illustrated treatment. The wholesale destruction of the Reformation period notwithstanding, it is surprising that Becket's enormous popularity is reflected only in this one single and fragmentary survival of such a book.

THE MANUSCRIPT

The manuscript of the illustrated Life of St Thomas Becket survives as a fragment only of four separate leaves. The pages measure about 303mm by 223mm and show signs of staining from glue and damp. Because vellum is a strong material, old leaves from unwanted manuscripts were sometimes in the past re-used by bookbinders for strengthening sewing and for lining the covers of bookbindings, and it seems likely that the Becket Leaves owe their preservation to the chance of having been pasted as padding into the covers of another book. These are the only four leaves of the manuscript which have ever been found. One has to say that it is possible, of course, that other pieces could lie still undetected and glued down in other bindings somewhere.

The known fragments were discovered in Belgium. In the 19th century they formed part of the vast library relating to the history of Courtrai assembled soon after the French Revolution by Jacques Goethals-Vercruysse (died 1838) and when his collection was presented to the city of Courtrai, the Becket Leaves, which did not form part of the library's theme of local topography, were retained by a collector's family and remained in their possession until 1986. The decades following the French Revolution formed a golden period for book buyers. Ancient libraries from suppressed monasteries were thrown onto the market much faster than they could be absorbed by public collections, and it is to the credit of energetic antiquarians such as Goethals-Vercruysse that certain monastic books and archives survived at all.

As no other copy of this verse Life of Becket is known, it is only by guesswork that we can reconstruct what the volume must have looked like. On the lower edges of two pages here are faint traces in mirror-writing from another fifteen lines of text offset at some time from facing pages. Irregular tears along the extreme inner edges of leaves 3 and 4 indicate with some certainty that these two separate sheets were once joined on a bifolium or pair of leaves. There is text missing before f.3 and after f.4, shadowily present in the offsets. Probably only one leaf came between ff.2 and 3, and perhaps the fragments formed the first, second, fourth and fifth leaves of a gathering of eight leaves, the usual unit in which medieval books were made up. If so, then at least one gathering preceded the first surviving leaf, and at least three more leaves followed it. This would seem to make textual sense: the story here is taken up to Becket's arrival back in England, and three subsequent leaves (six pictures) would be about right for the return into Canterbury, the confrontation with the knights, the murder itself, and perhaps Becket's canonisation.

The surviving fragment of the poem comprises 506 lines of octosyllabic rhyming verse. They are written in dark brown ink in two to three columns in a small and regular early gothic bookhand. Headings are in red. Small initials are painted in red or blue with contrasting penwork decoration. The format and the style of the text are very similar to those of a group of three other extant verse lives of saints composed towards the middle of the thirteenth century by the famous monk of St Albans, Matthew Paris, the chronicler and artist. These include the *Life of St Edward the Confessor,* now in Cambridge (fig. 10), and the *Lives of Sts Alban and Amphibalus,* now in Dublin (fig. 9). They are of similar size and illustrated like this with oblong pictures across the top of each page. Similarity of style does not prove authorship, but there are two tantalising medieval references telling of an illustrated book on Thomas Becket which Matthew Paris made. The first is in the 14th-century records of St Albans abbey praising Matthew who 'wrote and most elegantly illustrated the Lives of . . . the archbishops of Canterbury Thomas and Edmund'. The second reference is in the Dublin manuscript just cited which has the ownership inscription of Matthew Paris himself and which has flyleaf jottings in Matthew's own hand. One of these personal memoranda records that the Countess of Arundel now has the book on St Thomas the Martyr which (Matthew Paris noted of

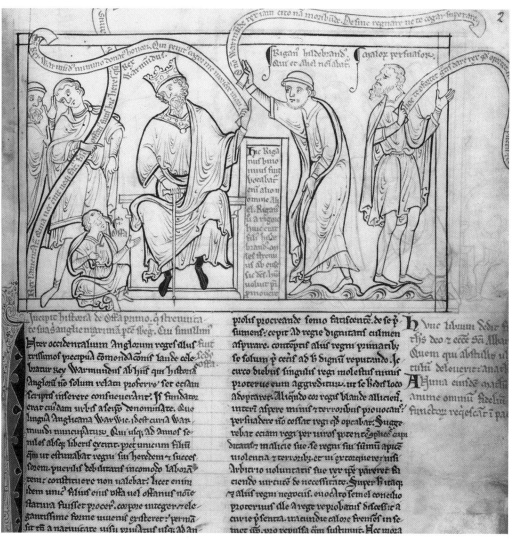

8 King Warmund of the West Angles contemplating his son Offa, blind and dumb in infancy. A drawing from Matthew Paris's Latin prose *Lives of the Offas,* executed about 1250. Both drawing and script are by the author's own hand. Cotton MS Nero D. i, f.2.

himself) *'transtuli et protraxi'*, apparently meaning which 'I translated and designed'. It is not known to survive; probably these four leaves are part of that lost text.

The style of illustration in the Becket Leaves has been associated with Matthew Paris ever since the leaves were first published in 1885. Matthew is one of the first English artists whose name is known and around whom a recognisable *oeuvre* can be reconstructed. He became a monk at St Albans in 1217 and died in 1259. By the thirteenth century, the writing and decorating of manuscripts was becoming a secular trade rather than being an almost exclusively monastic activity. Matthew Paris is remembered as one of the last truly monastic polymaths. He excelled in the technique of outline drawings tinted in areas of delicate coloured wash. It is very different from the more usual manuscript illumination made up of areas of thick coloured tempera and burnished gold, and it is ideally suited to the illustration of narrative. A century ago, every manuscript in this style was linked with

9 A scene from the martyrdom of St Alban. A coloured drawing illustrating Matthew Paris's French verse *Lives of Sts Alban and Amphibalus,* mid 13th century. Both drawing and script are attributed to the author. Dublin, Trinity College, MS E. i. 40, f.38v.

10 Edward the Confessor receiving news of the death of Harthacnut (left) and setting sail for England (right). A coloured drawing illustrating the French verse *Life of St Edward* attributed to Matthew Paris. This copy probably dates from about 1255–60. Cambridge, University Library, MS Ee. 3. 59, f.8v.

the famous name of Matthew Paris and was ascribed to what was called the 'school of St Albans'. More critical analysis over recent generations has taught us extreme caution. Coloured line drawings occur in English manuscripts back to the tenth century, and many of those that can be localised are demonstrably not from St Albans. Furthermore, enough survives in books which Matthew Paris himself owned and decorated (including the volume in Dublin) for his handwriting and his artistic style to be recognisable beyond reasonable doubt, and the script and illustrations of the Becket leaves are not, in fact, personal work of Matthew Paris. The style of the script and decoration in the Becket fragments suggest a date of around 1220–1240, consistent with the decades of Matthew's great activity. They have stylistic links with books which were at St Albans and with manuscripts which can be tentatively associated with early London workshops, a day's

Plate I
The earliest illustration of Becket's martyrdom. The four knights arrive at Becket's palace while the Archbishop sits at supper (above); the death of Becket and the penance of the four knights at his shrine (below).
About 1180. Cotton MS Claudius B. ii, f.214v.

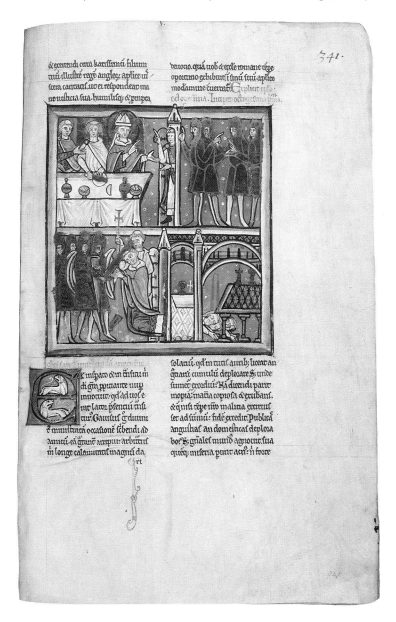

journey south of St Albans. Matthew Paris apparently supervised book production at his own abbey and probably at Westminster Abbey too. Though a monk, Matthew Paris was not a recluse and he knew Henry III personally. If he was the author of the life of St Thomas, as seems probable, the book could easily have been prepared under his direction by monks or professional artists in either royal abbey.

What seems likely is that Matthew Paris translated and devised illustrated verse lives of the saints. He himself would have sketched out designs for the illustrations. His own autograph copies, which he retained, would then act as the exemplars for the preparation of *de luxe* copies for presentation to noble recipients, often women apparently. The Becket Leaves give every appearance of being thoroughly professional skilful work but they may be only one remove from the author's sketchier autograph model. This is surely what Matthew Paris meant when he noted that he translated and prepared the text of which the Countess of Arundel has a copy, and the four leaves may be from that actual manuscript.

Plate II
The death of Becket.
Among the four knights,
Reginald Fitzurse is
distinguished by the bear
on his shield.
The cross-bearer has
traditionally been
identified as Becket's
biographer, Edward
Grim, who records that
he was wounded in the
struggle.
About 1200.
Harley MS 5102, f.32.

The recipient of Matthew Paris's text was Isabella de Warenne, daughter of the Earl of Surrey. In 1234 she became Countess of Arundel by her marriage to Hugh, Earl of Sussex and Arundel (died 1243). She outlived her husband by nearly 40 years, dying in 1282, and was buried at the Cistercian abbey she had founded at Marham in Norfolk. The nunnery was richly endowed by Isabella. It is possible that she gave them books. The Cistercians had an especial devotion to St Thomas Becket whom they sheltered in exile. One could imagine that at the Reformation a life of St Thomas might be transferred for safety from Norfolk to Flanders, perhaps to another Cistercian nunnery such as Groeninghe-lez-Courtrai which was suppressed in Courtrai in 1797 at the time Jacques Goethals-Vercruysse was buying up relics of local libraries. Such a hypothetical line of descent is possible, but it is quite without proof. What is certain is that when the pages came back into England in 1986 they were returning to their country of origin, and that without the spirited bidding of Mr Getty their return to England would have been extremely brief.

Plate III
The burial of Becket.
The martyr is laid to rest
by monks of Christ
Church cathedral priory,
robed in the vestments
which he wore at his
consecration and
wearing his archbishop's
pallium.
About 1200.
Harley MS 5102, f.17.

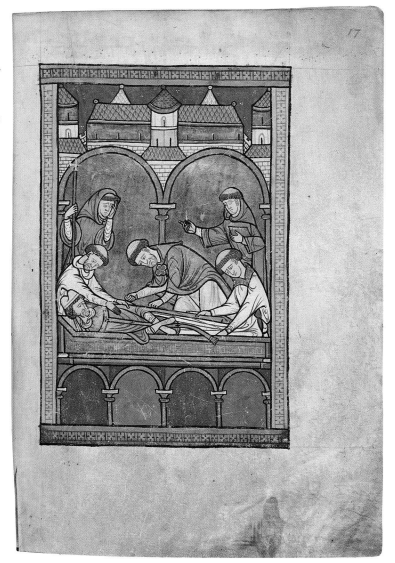

Plate IV The baptism of Becket's mother. A marginal illustration from Queen Mary's Psalter. Early 14th century. Royal MS 2 B. vii, f.289.

Plate V Becket consecrated Archbishop of Canterbury, 3 June 1162. A marginal illustration from Queen Mary's Psalter. Early 14th century. Royal MS 2 B. vii, f.290.

THE BECKET LEAVES

ex henr.   Icet toit angos li gurit eh 7 ei pleine   ti firmatur p ṁpio teiu / mo / ey tu / tur au / rem / apd ioue stuie / moz / tur / augi / ǒol   s ch.

Por le roi est grillez
De thomas tur li paientez
Hors de terre nest espartu
He li tounes ne li euchani
He la femme ben giline
Tient sun cufant a sa peine
He mangue fort du pulment
Punt seuri fu li ciuient
Viandes arret sanz sauni
Veille de nuitz uire de iurz
Qu aitz co li est de sustrir gref
Tendre sui nurri e suef
Tanr se met en gu desivese
Fl partant ky sun cors blesse
Trauailz ki ont auant duble
Qu aus lestat de sun cors truble
Repuer li cors sustenir
Ke li quers out en desir
Paiemne adle quee fade
Cuchez sen est par tant malade
En suen secrei confessur
Si mut lama par gun vedeur

Cumande par obedience
Kil uiure autrement eutneto
Cich ne uolt estre acuntraire
Qu aiz set cunseilz e cumandz faire
Si nun la uie cust perdue
Sa manere change e mue
Si set amesure ne fuch
De feblesce mortz genit
Qu aiz deu iad par sauctu
Fl auie e sante tendu
emuit li rois dengleterre
Tanz est iriez ne sez be faire
Triistie uoir de iur en un
Si un repruuer e desbonur
Qu ut est laidir e escharni
E maudit co pense li
Fl la postoile euuoir a dire
Ke trop dure eutreut celue
Facord mult desire e uetir
Kele nest faire mut sen detir
Qu essagers iuenent e uinit
Ki alez e repairer sunt

Par ses ieunes e ueraisunt
Veilles e afflictiuns
Febles est le quoz ad fade
Cuches sen est malade
Par force de obedience
Amenda puit cele abitinence
Eli apostoile respunt
Bile desturbe peche sunt
Qu aiz ne seruient legerement
Pes fort par cōmun asent
Si fuissent andui psent
Par ait seruient a tel par leuret
Si ensemble cuissent parle
Tost enteruient acorde
Qu aiz li rois ni asent pas
Ken semble soient il e thomas
Larcueuesq a co respunt
Ne place adeu kisar le rund
E pur nul mort suffir en croiz
Ke ni eusse la tierce uoiz
Par la pape par fauit crire
Purroit faut iugemēt seur

Alexand papa   3 th.

Li apostoiller bien entent
Ke tru pes saure ni apent
Si assemblez ni fuissent tivil
La pape e il e li voit
Auiui mande ken nule guise
Tant stoit ume sente iglise
Li mestag senuurt a tant
Qur eururer e manaeant

Quant pes su a honur mise
Entre lempure e seinte iglise
E tant sait ke li emperes
E par force e par prieres
Ke de citer e de tresoz
Petiu sist plener e uedoz
La pape de france sen part
Ki mult pe ke deul la gart
Ki tant li su eertein resut
E n sun peril e sun esriu
E quant sun chemin aeuit
Li arceuesq le eunduit
Esq a burger la returne
Pur le partir tire e murne

Quant pes su a honur mise
Entre lempure e seinte iglise
La pape de france sen part
Ki mur pe ke deus la gart
Li arceuesq lad eunuoie
Esq en burger la tire
La eunge pur e sen returne
Lun e lautre sen par murne
La pape nauers Rume droit
Li arceuesq benoit
A pirs ele departie
Hele uir une en eeste uie
Larceuesq ki a pun tremun
Repaire v seur tapi
E meine solitaure uie
E u estr... e estudie
E u teure e en mraisun
V eille e sottremplatiun
V murs aprent desçuiture
Kar il i met entente e eture
Haprist tant auant meint an
Cq sur tost eruue en out sathan

Li enuiue e li engrez
Ki tost destuiba eele per
Nuie ke puet deueniir
Ke ne sier sa pes tenir
Au tirant henri mult peise
Ke laureuesq est tant a eise
Ki sen ur ke nule lauiue
D iluee euuen bil le remue
Au chapistre de eistaus
Cq ande bil ne li sunt leaus
Ki sun mortel enemi
E ume tel solaz e tel arbri
Cib ki mun enemi aeort
A moi honur ne bienne uort
Ki mun enemi auance
A moi sait mal e desturbance
S il nel saeent amender
Cq ultiur touldra giant auer
D e lur graunge e maisune
Petuine e possessiune
D unt mut uint en englesie
E cib de perte nuiie ke seie

Ou cuncil escrier sen part
entr encuntre chescune part
z demandent la benetzun
uit chescun a sun cumpaignun
eez le leal advocat
cu ke sul pur li cumbat
dit nentent mie tumenr
ces par un cumun parlement
suissent cumun tut trei
arceuesq il elu rei
ui parle lad e pur ueu
ensemble sunt tut trei uenu
dune e dautre part grant gent
i pur la pes i sunt present
i rois henri uint uolentiers
ar dui li curent messagiers
e larceuesq seint deti
e metuint tut en sa mai
uant tuit furent assemble
li roi li cuntre e li lettre
arceuesq; sen humilie

spek le rei henri se phe
li dit. Deu sire roi
mendez sil uus plest a moi
a cause tute a uus cumand
autes entr uostre cumand
resture a uostre plaisir
abandun a grant laisir
auk lonur de deu
ue li roi henris semblant
lui est uer ke nest leun
quant blesce se sent dragun
dit hai tant mal asist
es bien u par moi es mis
Puis sest turnez au roi de france
e dit oez grant dereuance
um ore muet descord e fusine
ar wenelar e par sofisme
li tut muer sul le descord
tut fait entendre kan tort
ar par test mot. sauk lonur
e deu nus met tut en errur

a reinept̄ roꝭ eboꝛ · z ex h. iunioꝛ · ex hur p̄ · ex hm̄ filiꝰ eiꝰ

Ki pes se tient e patience	Truit henrit grante e ome	Li peret li fiſt ioie ſi grant
He remaudut gumdit ne tere	De englerere la curume	Ka ceuir li fu ſergaunt
Vn de ſes clers li dut beu ſire	A ſun fir eſne henri	Coiant pluſurſ gei
Li muſt bad nun martire	Sepentant ſu puis e marri	Ke ſul fu voil roſne henri
Fu vaire hut de cuncorde	Li prelar deuerſbie Roger	Ke mie eſt ki oine ſeru
Ke ala uerne ſe acorde	A tort lempuſt aturuper	Dunt mut apreſ ſe repenti
Kar par martire ert uaue	Roger deuerſbie iſu	oꝙ ur ſendolut en apreſ
Bien le vuit deuin ſme	Li arceueſques auneu	Kar poi dura lamur e pes
par uſe moꝛt ſeinte iglite	Leueſꝗ fu de lundres la	A preſpoi dure ſen diſlut
Tunqueria pes e franchiſe	Liſt de ... iua	Kil auꝑere guerre mut
Larceueſꝗ a ẽ reſpun	Li eueſꝗ ꝗ ſaleſbur	Co ſu au cumencement
Co pleiſe a ẽu ki ſtable mund	Cuntre loꝛun de canterebure	Le pmier enuchement
Pur ſa tire ſeure	Que larceueſꝗ eſt tut toi	Du perche lu toi henri
Et tur ſun regne conſiner	Et urent a cuunel le roi	Ki ſert thomaſ tant pur ſun
Su fir kert eir alwemuſt	Henri le roſne laſ liue	**baun** li plaiſt de canterebure
Henri li roi uieuꝛ cuꝛtreſ	oꝛ en aium̄ meſquentuir	loi recunter e oire
Dieuꝰ pluſur aꝛ ꝗ greuer	a feſte ſure plenerement	oꝙ ur ſe tint deſperſone
Co ... urndir e enames	**L**du mang eurent guant gent	E mut ſun bonur blaſce
Lauouure e la ſranchiſe	Le pere ſiſt au fir guant feſte	La dignete de ſa iglite
Alarceueſꝗ e ſa iglite	He oimeſ en chantun nien geſte	**Q**ur deſucuibre e maumiſe
Tante gene reſtoir baune	Ki fut de ruche hom ſeru	Aſet leſ enuiſe chaſtier
Dе clerge e de cheualerie	Cum fu li roſne rois henri.	E par la pape amoneſter

4

alexand p̄

Column 1

E prier au comencement
D e cele emp̄se z osement
Q̄ dul ni eust mest prier
H e cumandement de per̄
D esteit de ami ṅ uersin
K il ne fuissent au roi enclin
L i apostoille suuent
C umande e p̄e ducement
K il ne facent cuntre la feise
D u regne ne de sein̄te iglise
C is tindrent tut en despit
E eschiurent sun escrit
T ut cuntre lur cunscience
E cuntre sein̄te obedience
A la fin bien co parut
K a deu lur oure pas ne plut
Q̄ ilst enuint mal e enclibrir
P ar le istme roi coroner
S anc de arceuesc̄ espandu
A utres eueisc̄ suspendu
E li autre escumenger
E cunfundur e exiller
E guerre entre fiz e per̄
Q̄ eue mortele e amere
E n iiii.lef anz de sa uuente
E sanz pur plut u mem̄s de sute
Q̄ urut li iouur toit henri
D uire ueuz e tourel sun mari
D e sa beinte de salargesce
D e sa bunte e sa pruesce
V emp̄rroit mut dure
L Q̄ auc co seroit hors de matire
 la nouele est espandue
E par terres tost seue
D u coruncment henri
L i iouure ki tant deli
T ut aferme tut acumpli
P oit su clamer li roit henri
L i iounes ki tant fu beuls
E pruz e frans iuuenceuls

Column 2

L arceuesq̄ quant lot e suet
K est merueille si li greft
la pape sect pleint e mande
E amender le cumande
E cist mande kil escumine
T uz du cunseil e la cuine
Q̄ uant lot oïre sein̄t thomas
O il fust irez ne esmueil pas
K ar a sa p̄sone ajut
L e rreal coruneme̅t
E sil ne peut estre p̄seint
S uiuaut par sun aseiureme̅t
Q̄ auc ore su autreme̅t e pit
H i su present ne cunseil q̄
P uis kil out tut cest ateint
A l apostoille sect pleint
D e ceuc de sa subiecttun
K i unt fait tel mesp̄sun
A lur pere e lur p̄elat
K i sul pur euc tuz cumbat
E ki siurent quil pire tut
E del roi mortel cururt

Column 3

Q̄ uant li apostoille en su cert
Q̄ uel mal unt ia fait li culurt
A sein̄t thomas otiert poer
D e suspendre e escumuner
K ar plut li greue cest destri
E psecutiun du uei
p lut li greue ceu destui
K e la greuance lu roi
p lut sen deur e plut seiunaie
K ar co est cum coup sur plaie
E ntre douc moeles gist thomas
Q uant baut le pint e nui li bas
B reusemble de briment le gram
K i muluz est a faire p̄ui
L a pape qut lot uint en esmut
E du rogne de france tut
D el autre part li roit de frince
p rie ben p̄uine uengance
L a pape cum il sun seruise
E amur ueut sanz feintise
W illame li p̄elat de saint
D es mauc sein̄t thoma doillant

Verai li prudom le nout garniu
A tant regarde e uoir uenir
Cil hun qui de kil eir desir
Fet demander e fet uenir
Sire dib mister nest pas ci
He uieng pas fret demand ci
Einz uus di un mandement
De part le cunte iste e dolent
Kel uus puet tant les met dire
A turner sunt pur uul ocire
E aduersers grant assemblee
De la la mer cunt u armee
Quant ad le mandement oi
Tut les e baud li respundi
E engleterre sui aler prest
Feint sui li p tant passer les
Tuir est ke cantorebire
Cos ore sun pastur desire
Set anz ad ke io ni fui
Ki du liu arceuesq sui
A tant regarde ul la riue
E vit une nef se ariue
Hom demande qui est uenue

Milun sen uient bret fiant
Au passageur de Wistsant
Sire uoler ke uoirs uus cunte
De part mun seignu le cunte
De Buloinne Armee gent
De la mer par mel uul atent
Si nuuele fusd seue
Del arceuesq en engletire
Cib dicut ne uolent tere
Ki disoient espessement
Ki uendront nouelement
Uint grant ioie euuer e bau
Qz ait un de cul une part les riaiz
Ki dist retraez uul chautiefs
Semble il u lunges keste uifs
Del cheualler une grant rute
De la uul atent sant dute
Ki pierz sunt e apareiller
De uus ocire qui iuendrent
Qur cid la terre esmeue
En uire p meire uenue
A chesun ture su u merent
Larceuesq e suert tur rettrer

Par une nef keb ariuee
E si sa parole acertee
Uient cib bariuez sunt
Cent armee mil de brunt
Guerre qui ariuerez
Ke soiez tur tost detrencher
Par larceuesq Boger
Eupreistes de aurucep
C les euesques ke auez
Suspenduz e escuminer
Ou les cueilse bi rsunt
Ki cunt uul sunt tut de brunt
Gerald de Warenne ceb
Li uisquens ceruelse preb
E randouf de bive ki la
Li arceuesqz escuminia
Os grant cupaigne armee
Tut ensemble afiancee
Atendent sur la marine
Kiuir e nuit guetter ne fine
Se serez plust ost ariuez
Ke pendoz e destrecher seb esbaie
Uant ture sa cpaigne co or uuit

Folio 1r. Two scenes:

(1) HENRY II SENDS INTO EXILE ALL THOMAS BECKET'S RELATIONS who flee to take refuge at Pontigny Abbey in Burgundy. Henry sits on his throne, holding a scroll '*Exullet tota propago vulgaris Thome et ei presentetur*', while two soldiers carry out his orders (the biblical parallel with Herod and the Innocents is only thinly veiled) and forcibly threaten four men and a woman clutching a baby in her arms; this last detail derives from Herbert of Bosham who witnessed '*parvuli etiam incunabulis*' among the exiles.

(2) THOMAS BECKET LIES IN PONTIGNY ABBEY, ILL FROM EXCESSIVE FASTING. The archbishop lies on a simple bed with its hangings hooked back as a doctor with a book anxiously examines a specimen flask and holds out little hope that Thomas will survive, '*Infirmatur pre nimio jejunio apud Pontiniacum, sinisterque rumor auditus auget dolorem*'.

Folio 1v.

THOMAS BECKET TAKES LEAVE OF POPE ALEXANDER III in the autumn of 1165. Alexander had attempted to mediate in the dispute between Thomas and the King, and when the Pope returned to Rome, Thomas accompanied him as far as Bourges before taking his leave and returning to Pontigny. The scene here shows the Pope, preceded by his cross-bearer and followed by members of his court, hugging Thomas and exhorting him to stand firm in his struggle.

Folio 2r. Two scenes:

(1) THOMAS BECKET PRONOUNCES THE SENTENCE OF EXCOMMUNICATION ON ALL HIS ENEMIES and dashes a candle to the ground. This takes place in the summer of 1166, and Becket excommunicates all those in England who have committed offences against the property or persons of Becket's followers. The guilty here lurch back in horror and dismay.

(2) THOMAS BECKET ARGUES HIS CASE BEFORE HENRY II AND LOUIS VII. The characters of the protagonists are very well drawn. The meeting took place at Montmirail on 6 January 1169. Henry II, with all his old cunning, attempts to be reasonable and is seen here counting certain demands on his fingers, as his courtiers wait anxiously behind. Louis VII, appointed by the Pope as his representative, is caught with his loyalties on both sides. The boys in the foreground are simply shouting abuse. Thomas Becket, however, agrees to everything asked of him, adding the clause which effectively negates his acquiescence as he makes it, 'saving the honour of God', '*Oblatis adquiesco salvo honore dei*'.

Folio 2v.

THOMAS BECKET DEPARTS FROM HENRY II AND LOUIS VII. Negotiations have broken down. The two kings ride off from Montmirail with gestures of frustration and fury, and the royal guards make jokes at the Archbishop's expense. Becket, however, joins 'the '*vulgus*' (as it is called here), the common people who beg for his blessing.

Folio 3r. Two scenes:

(1) THE CORONATION OF THE YOUNG HENRY in Westminster Abbey. This was a major political blunder by Henry II. As a partial solution to the problem of his successor, Henry II had proposed to crown his son, the younger Henry ('*Rex. H.iunior*' here), as a kind of co-monarch in his father's lifetime. The practice was unprecedented in England but, more importantly, a coronation could not take place without the Archbishop of Canterbury. The coronation is shown taking place here at the hands of Roger of Pont l'Evêque, Archbishop of York and Thomas Becket's hated rival, attended by Gilbert, Bishop of London, Jocelin, Bishop of Salisbury, and other bishops. It happened on 14 June 1170.

(2) THE CORONATION BANQUET in Westminster Palace. We see the table laid out for a feast with food and wine and implements, and the minstrel lad in the foreground. In a symbolic gesture, Henry II serves the royal cup to his son whom he salutes as King of England. A guest holds a scroll '*Ecce maiestas nimis inclinata*'. The banquet is said to have been of enormous proportions and extravagance.

Folio 3v. Two scenes:

(1) THE NEWS REACHES THOMAS BECKET who is outraged at this deliberate insult to his person and to his office as Archbishop and head of the Church in England. The messenger has hastened with a letter for Becket telling him of the coronation, and has not paused to change from his travelling clothes (and seems to have a few waves of the Channel still under his feet). Becket claps his hand to his brow.

(2) THOMAS BECKET SENDS A FORMAL COMPLAINT TO THE POPE. Four years before, Alexander III had specifically forbidden the bishops to crown the young Henry, and Becket now felt he had finally caught out Henry II on a legal technicality.

Folio 4r.

THOMAS BECKET PREPARES TO SAIL FOR ENGLAND to end his six-year exile. As he and a companion walk along the beach at Wissant, near Boulogne, a man appears with a money bag. Thomas mistakes him for the ticket collector for the boat ('*collector nauli*' in the caption above the miniature – 'the fare collector') and dismisses him. In fact, he is Milo, agent of the Count of Boulogne, who has come to warn him not to sail to England as his enemies are waiting to kill him there. However, the boat from England is already bobbing on the shoreline, and Thomas Becket sets sail on 30 November 1170.

Folio 4v.

THOMAS BECKET ARRIVES BACK IN ENGLAND, landing at Sandwich, one of his own properties, rather than at Dover where a retinue of knights was awaiting him. Even at Sandwich there is quite a crowd. The poor and the lame struggle out in a little boat and in the water to be blessed by the holy Archbishop. On the shore are the '*Regales et Brokenses*', the royal henchmen and the men of Randulph de Broc, the powerful Kentish landowner who had been pillaging Becket's possessions. There is at least one bishop among the sinister welcome party, and one soldier relents enough to warn Thomas Becket against coming ashore.

From this moment onwards, as all early biographers were quick to stress, the Becket story would take on an echo of the Gospels. Becket's triumphant procession from the coast to Canterbury is like the Entry into Jerusalem. Charges are brought against him, and Becket refuses to recant. He is taken out for a last supper, and is martyred in Canterbury Cathedral, four weeks after the last incident shown here.

Suggestions for further reading

F. BARLOW, *Thomas Becket,* London 1986. This is the most recent study of the saint.

P. MEYER, *Fragments d'une vie de Saint Thomas de Cantorbéry* (Société des anciens textes français), Paris 1885. This remains the only edition of the French verse text that appears on the Becket Leaves.

N. J. MORGAN, *Early Gothic Manuscripts (1): 1190–1250* (A Survey of Manuscripts Illuminated in the British Isles, vol. 4), London and Oxford 1982. The Becket Leaves are no. 61 in this catalogue, where a bibliography is given.

N. J. MORGAN, 'Matthew Paris, St Albans, London, and the leaves of the "Life of St Thomas Becket"', *The Burlington Magazine,* vol. cxxx, no. 1019, February 1988.

R. VAUGHAN, *Matthew Paris,* Cambridge 1958. The book includes a discussion of the saints' lives attributed to Matthew.

B. WARD, *Miracles and the Medieval Mind,* London 1982, revised edition 1987. Becket's cult and miracles are examined in detail.